Cave Painting to E-mail
The Evolution of Writing

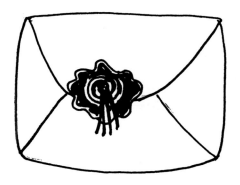

by Elizabeth West

illustrated by Ilene C. Richard

Harcourt

Orlando   Boston   Dallas   Chicago   San Diego

Visit *The Learning Site!*

www.harcourtschool.com

Writing Has a History

Writing is just about everywhere in the modern world. If we walk down any urban street, a barrage of signs, advertisements, posters, menus, and other announcements greets us. If we turn on a television set, we are bombarded by news headlines, titles, actors' names, maps, and charts. Even without television, letters, magazines, newspapers, books, and messages from friends and family come to us. Keeping in touch with others has never been easier than it is today; however, the materials and processes that have made such written communication possible did not develop overnight.

Written language has had a long history. People from many cultures participated in this history, sharing one common goal: communication. Almost as soon as people learned to write, they looked for ways to speed up the process. To do this, they invented new writing materials and machines, including everything from paper and pens to modern word processors. The e-mail messages you send and receive are part of a history that began thousands of years ago.

Early Writing

No one knows exactly when writing started or how it came about; however, we do know that people have always expressed themselves through symbols. Cave dwellers painted on the rock walls of their caves and carved symbols into flat stones and animal horns. The purpose of some early writing is as unclear as its origins. Were early people recording history— or just expressing themselves? We may never know.

The earliest methods of written communication must have had few readers, since the readers had to come to the writing. To read cave symbols, for instance, someone had to enter the cave. Later, writers began to work with materials that were portable, allowing them to bring their writing to their readers. Sumerians, for example, wrote on clay tablets. These tablets were small enough to carry by hand from place to place; the tablets could also be stored—and read by later generations. Archaeologists have found many of these tablets in the Middle East, some dating as far back as 3500 B.C.

No one is sure exactly how writing spread, but archaeologists have determined that writing advanced quickly around the globe. Whether by coincidence or by some as-yet-undiscovered cause, writing sprang up in several places simultaneously. The earliest forms of writing contained illustrations of people and objects. In time, writing systems included symbols that stood for words. Still later, people developed symbols that represented syllables, and finally symbols that stood for sounds. About 1700 B.C., the world received its first real alphabet, from which originated every major alphabet we now use.

Today, there are hundreds of different alphabets. They contain an average of 28 signs, although the Cambodian alphabet has 72. Not only do the letters in different alphabets look different, but the methods of writing them vary as well. Although people read and write most alphabets (such as ours) from left to right, in some alphabets the words go in different directions; for example, Arabic and Hebrew are written from right to left, while Chinese, Japanese, and Korean are written vertically.

Early Writing Surfaces

At first people wrote on writing surfaces such as stone and baked clay, but these surfaces took up a lot of space, and they were heavy. Imagine trying to carry a bag full of clay tablets to a distant city!

Around 3000 B.C., the Egyptians discovered how to make sheets of soft, flat writing material similar to paper. They called the material *papyrus* because it consisted of fibers from the papyrus plant, a type of reed that flourished along the Nile. They used papyrus sheets individually or pasted together in scrolls.

Although scrolls were a great improvement over tablets, reading a scroll was cumbersome. The reader first had to unroll the scroll and flatten it out. Usually, after reading one section, the reader rolled up that portion to protect it. After reading the entire scroll, the reader rewound it for the next person. Scrolls are still used today, although mainly for ceremonial or religious occasions.

For hundreds of years, writing was restricted to wealthy and powerful people. Religious leaders, rulers, and nobles could read and write, but common people could not. In fact, those in power often forbade the teaching of reading to the masses, because reading allows people to share ideas. Those in power feared the consequences of letting the common people read viewpoints that could undermine the leaders' power.

Parchment

The second century B.C. marked the emergence in Europe of parchment, a writing material made from animal skins, most often from sheep and goats. To prepare the surface of an animal skin for writing, someone had to split the skin and rub it with a variety of abrasive powders; only then was the surface suitable for ink or paint.

Parchment had several advantages over papyrus: Both sides of a sheet were suitable for writing; parchment was pliable, so the sheets could be folded into books; and finally, people could reuse parchment, since the writing could be rubbed or scraped off.

For centuries, most fine books were handwritten by scribes on pages of parchment. Most scribes worked for a church or a ruler. Churches wanted scribes to write prayers, psalms, and religious texts, while rulers asked for proclamations. Although the process of creating these manuscripts was painstaking, the results were often spectacularly beautiful. Some documents were illuminated, or decorated with gold and bright colors. Miniature portraits and illustrations adorned others.

By the time Europeans invented parchment, the Chinese were already making paper. Before using paper, the Chinese had written on bamboo or silk—but bamboo was heavy and silk was costly, so the Chinese experimented and discovered how to make paper.

Paper

Like papyrus, the first paper consisted of vegetable fibers. The first paper also included old fishnets, mulberry fibers, and rags, while later papers often contained cotton or linen. Rag paper, as such paper was called, was strong, smooth, lightweight, and durable. For years, rag paper was the most convenient writing surface, but it was available only in China. Furthermore, the Chinese kept their manufacturing processes secret.

Over time, however, good inventions have a way of circulating, and the recipe for paper was no exception. By the year 600, the Japanese and Koreans also knew how to manufacture rag paper, and soon the Arabs learned the secret, too. The Arabs carried this knowledge to Europe, and within a few centuries, the Europeans had their own paper mills.

Paper quickly became the dominant writing material in the world. Papyrus disappeared from use, as did the documents written on papyrus, which decomposed in the moist European climate, burned in fires, or were otherwise lost. Since parchment required time-consuming preparation and quantities of animal skins, it became a material used mainly for ceremonial or official documents.

In the 1450s, the invention of the mechanical printing press revolutionized both reading and writing. The mechanical press made books abundant and available to everyone, not just to the upper classes. The new technology also created a phenomenal demand for paper, since printers could now produce books in large numbers.

A scarcity of paper resulted from a shortage of rags. Paper makers needed large quantities of rags, and the new demand for paper consumed all the readily available rags. At one point, the shortage was so severe that desperate paper makers started scavenging for rags on the streets or in dumps; others even tried using the bandages wrapped around Egyptian mummies. Clearly, the world needed paper that could be produced from a more readily available material.

That material turned out to be nearby and very abundant: trees. In the nineteenth century, new manufacturing methods allowed paper makers to turn wood pulp into paper. Wood pulp paper does not last as long as fabric-based papers, but it is much less expensive to manufacture. Today, most paper is made from wood pulp. Much of this pulp comes directly from trees, but more and more comes from recycled waste paper to help preserve standing trees.

I found it first!

Early Writing Tools

Early cave dwellers probably used their fingers as writing tools, dipping their fingers in juice or blood and then writing. The Sumerians developed a wedge-shaped stick called a stylus, which they pressed into soft clay to make triangular markings. Later, they baked the soft clay tablets and hardened them in the sun to make them durable.

Later, Egyptian writers used pens fashioned from hollow reeds. Writers would cut the reeds, shape the ends into pen points, and use them for writing on papyrus. Since the reed tip was flexible, it did not puncture the surface of the papyrus. When a pen broke, a writer could just walk outside and harvest another reed.

The Chinese wrote on paper with brushes made from animal hair, while Europeans used quill pens made from feathers. Like reeds, quills were hollow and could hold some ink inside; however, quills were more flexible, did not break as easily, and drew elegant lines. Writers usually owned several different sizes, from large turkey quills to small crow quills. Quills had one major drawback, however: With time, they became brittle and splintered. Once again, a new invention solved the problem.

Portable Tools

Mass-produced steel pen points revolutionized writing in the 1780s. Metal pen points were not new, but advances in technology now allowed large-scale manufacturing of these items. Pen points became cheaper; as a result, pens flooded the market, creating a new interest in handwriting, or "penmanship." Students took classes in which they practiced writing beautiful script in copybooks, which featured examples of beautiful writing for students to copy over and over.

Steel pens had fine points that were split into two pieces. If a writer drew the pen lightly across a page, it made a delicate line; if the writer pressed harder, the split widened to create a broader line. By alternately pressing and then releasing pressure, the writer could control the shape of the line as well as its direction. These shaped lines could create beautiful documents, but the pens did have a major disadvantage: writers constantly had to dip them into ink because they ran out quickly.

A few decades later, fountain pens—so called because their ink kept flowing like water in a fountain—carried their own ink supply inside. Fountain pens were an instant success, and they ruled the market until the 1950s, when ballpoint pens became popular. Like fountain pens, ballpoints carry their own ink, but they do not need refilling, and most are disposable. Every ballpoint pen has a thin tube of ink inside it. A tiny ball bearing covers the end of this tube, so when a writer drags the pen across the paper, friction turns the ball, which picks up ink as it turns.

Pre-Twentieth-Century Materials

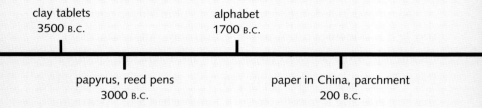

clay tablets
3500 B.C.

alphabet
1700 B.C.

papyrus, reed pens
3000 B.C.

paper in China, parchment
200 B.C.

Desk Tools

The first pens were created for people who could see, but the first typewriters were invented to help the blind. These early machines produced braille, a writing system composed of raised dots. These machines led to print typewriters.

Some early typewriters were as large as pianos, and many were inconvenient to use. The first typewriters typed only capital letters; subsequent models used separate keyboards for uppercase and lowercase letters.

Until the late 1880s, when new "shift-key" typewriters allowed typists to use a single keyboard, typing was a tedious process. Now the operator merely had to shift, or move, a key to make a letter uppercase or lowercase. Early keyboards were not uniform, but the QWERTY keyboard, named for the first six letters of the top row, quickly became the standard. (Check out a computer keyboard for the *Q-W-E-R-T-Y* keys on the top row.) The designer arranged the keyboard, not for speed, but to keep the keys from jamming if someone typed rapidly. Although other keyboards allow people to type faster, no arrangement has yet replaced the QWERTY keyboard.

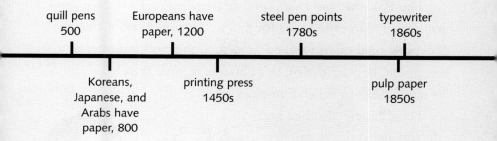

quill pens
500

Europeans have
paper, 1200

steel pen points
1780s

typewriter
1860s

Koreans,
Japanese, and
Arabs have
paper, 800

printing press
1450s

pulp paper
1850s

Writer Mark Twain was fascinated by the typewriter and became one of its first purchasers. He liked to tell people, "I was the first person in the world to apply the typewriter to literature." His enthusiasm for the machine probably helped make it more popular. Today, many people use a word processor instead of a typewriter. Unlike typewriters, word processors allow writers to create, edit, and save documents electronically.

Getting the Word Out: Early Postal Systems

Private messengers, called couriers, delivered the earliest written messages. Governments—not private citizens—used most of these early systems. The ancient Egyptians had a courier system of foot messengers and boats. Couriers also delivered the clay tablets used in the Middle East.

Around 500 B.C., the Greek historian Herodotus described the courier system of the Persians, which included various stations, or posts, each about a day's ride from one another. According to Herodotus, nothing interfered with the deliveries of the riders; they traveled despite "snow or rain, or heat, or...darkness of night."

The Romans had two postal systems, one reserved for government use and the other for private citizens. Within the city of Rome, mail often reached its destination within hours of being sent; beyond the metropolitan area, mail traveled about 50 miles a day to other European cities.

The Chinese also had an effective delivery system: by the thirteenth century, it included 10,000 stations and 300,000 horses. Couriers carried most local mail on foot, but they used horses for urgent messages or for those going great distances.

The English used the first adhesive postage stamps in 1840. Before that, the person who received the mail had to pay the transportation fee. Within a few decades, most countries began offering official postal service.

U.S. Mail

The first mail route in this country, between Boston and New York, started in 1673. The road that the messengers traveled was called the Boston Post Road.

At first, the service was expensive, unreliable, and inconvenient; messengers delivered mail only to post offices—not to homes. Later, as the new nation grew, so did its postal service, and within a few decades, mail service reached from one side of the country to the other. Sometimes mail arrived by boat, sometimes it arrived by horse or stage, and eventually it arrived by train.

Toward the end of the nineteenth century, people in large cities received mail at their homes. Thirty years later, "rural free delivery" brought mail delivery to homes in rural areas as well. Within twenty years after that, the law required homes to have mailboxes. Today, the United States postal system is the largest in the world.

Newer Methods

Although delivery time may be uncertain, letters are fun to receive. Handwritten letters often reflect the sender's personality and setting. Historians like letters written by famous people or those that tell about historical events. Paper letters will probably never disappear completely.

Electronic Communication

Today, if you have a home computer with a modem, you can send and receive e-mail or faxes from home. With adult supervision, you might also enter a chat room to have an online conversation; the other person could be next door or in another country. Conversations that take place in chat rooms are an interactive way of sending written messages. They feel almost like talking, because people can read what you type and respond instantly.

As people communicate in new ways, new problems arise. For example, with e-mail, people can easily send fake messages. They can pretend to be someone else when they send mail, and their messages can be hard to trace, since no handwriting or postmark points to the real sender. Electronic transmission does, however, leave an electronic trail. Experts can follow this trail to find senders who use e-mail to break laws.

Please call home

New methods and new problems create new tools. These tools will shape the communication of the future. No matter how far we advance, however, we will always have one thing in common with our ancestors: the basic need to communicate.